HEALTHY HEART COOKBOOK

BEVERLEY PIPER

SIMON & SCHUSTER
A VIACOM COMPANY

First published in Great Britain by Simon & Schuster Ltd, 1995
A Viacom Company

Simon & Schuster Ltd
West Garden Place
Kendal Street
London W2 2AQ

Design: Green Moore Lowenhoff
Typesetting: Stylize
Photography: Karl Adamson
Styling: Maria Kelly
Food preparation: Wendy Lee

Weight Watchers Publications Manager: Delia Bintley
Weight Watchers Publications Assistant: Celia Whiston

A CIP catalogue record is available from the British Library

ISBN 0-671-71954-8

Printed and bound in the United Kingdom by Print Wright Limited, Ipswich

For each cookbook sold through Weight Watchers Meetings, Weight Watchers (UK) Ltd. will donate 50p to British Heart Foundation Trading Ltd., a wholly owned trading subsidiary of British Heart Foundation (Registered Charity No. 225971), to which it covenants all of its taxable profits.

Pictured on the front cover: Spicy Glazed Vegetables (page 23)

Recipe notes:
Egg size is medium (size 3), unless otherwise stated.
Vegetables are medium-size, unless otherwise stated.
It is important to use proper measuring spoons, not cutlery, for spoon measures.
1 tablespoon = 15 ml; 1 teaspoon = 5 ml.
Dried herbs can be substituted for fresh ones, but the flavour may not always be as good. Halve the fresh-herb quantity stated in the recipe.

Vegetarian recipes:
These symbols show which recipes are suitable for vegetarians.

(V) shows the recipe is vegetarian

(V) shows the recipe has a vegetarian option

Contents

Foreword

by Heather Waring, Education Manager of the British Heart Foundation

Heart and circulatory disease is Britain's biggest killer, causing nearly half of all deaths in the nation. Although not all heart problems can be blamed on lifestyle, an estimated one–third of deaths due to coronary heart disease are linked to an unhealthy diet. The health of your heart is more in your control than you think.

The British Heart Foundation has been fighting heart disease for over 30 years. In hospitals and universities throughout the country we fund vital research into the causes, diagnosis, treatment and prevention of heart disease. By buying this book and encouraging your friends and family to do the same you will be helping in the fight against heart disease. By using this cookbook and taking your own steps towards a healthier heart you can help us even more!

Heather Waring

Get Heart-Smart

'Eating to your heart's content' is a well-used phrase which we should all begin to take a bit more literally. After all, the heart is the body's most important organ and works hard, pumping blood to every organ, muscle and limb. However, coronary heart disease is now the number one killer in the UK, accounting for one–third of all deaths each year. And as the chances of men and women developing heart disease are more or less equal for those over the age of 50, heart disease is no longer a concern primarily for men. In fact, over 76,000 women each year are killed by coronary heart disease and thousands more suffer from angina and other heart-related illnesses.

But the good news is that heart disease is largely preventable. By maintaining a healthy lifestyle now, you will keep your heart in good condition and prevent problems from arising in later years. As the state of your heart is reflected by the rest of your well-being, getting (and keeping) fit is the key to prevention. And as heart disease is linked closely to diet, this is one of the most significant areas where we can make some positive lifestyle changes. High blood cholesterol levels are known to be a major contributing factor to heart disease and can be reduced through dietary changes, as you'll read in the following pages.

Although everybody should be concerned about their cholesterol level, it's particularly important for people who are overweight, smoke or for those with a family history of heart disease. Alarmingly, 7 out of 10 adults in the UK have a blood cholesterol reading above the desirable level of 5.2 mmol per litre, so it's well worth having it checked periodically. Many doctors' surgeries and medical clinics offer cholesterol tests which are simple, quick and accurate.

Contrary to some people's thinking, maintaining a healthy lifestyle is neither difficult nor boring. And to prove it, in association with the British Heart Foundation, Weight Watchers have brought you this colourful cookbook with some simple advice along with 30 Calorie-counted recipes (including Weight Watchers Selections). So with the inspiration of some delicious dishes, you will soon be able to cook and eat to your *true* heart's content!

10 Easy Steps to a Healthy Heart

1. Stop Smoking

Smoking is one of the most easily prevented causes of ill health. Smokers are far more likely to develop heart disease, bronchial problems and lung cancer, while women who smoke and take oral contraceptives are at even greater risk of heart disease. Nicotine causes the arteries to constrict, forcing the heart to work harder, while the carbon monoxide produced by smoking tobacco reduces the amount of oxygen carried by the blood. Moreover, smoking inhibits the tastebuds and to compensate for this, smokers are prone to over-indulge in their use of salt and sugar, which is bad news for both heart and waistline. All things considered, smoking hasn't got much to recommend it. A quick word of advice to those smokers who are hesitant to quit because they're afraid of putting on weight. Some people do gain a few pounds when they first give up smoking. If you are attending Weight Watchers Meetings, ask your leader for a copy of Weight Watchers booklet *Stopping Smoking and Losing Weight* – it's packed with information and advice.

2. Reduce Your Blood Cholesterol Level

Many people are confused by the term cholesterol and assume that it is an entirely bad thing which we can avoid simply by not eating foods such as eggs. As I've explained below, cholesterol levels are most effectively lowered by cutting back on the type and amount of fats one eats. To appreciate why this is so, it helps to understand what cholesterol actually is.

Blood cholesterol is a fat-like substance found in our blood which is produced by our bodies and is essential for the proper functioning of many body systems. Dietary cholesterol is that which we consume in foods of animal origin, but because it is made within the body as well, we do not really need it in our diet. This 'extra' cholesterol which we consume does not have a great effect on blood cholesterol levels, but the type and amount of fat which we eat do. Saturated fats increase the amount of blood cholesterol in the blood circulation. Excesses of fatty deposits can build up along the artery walls. The arteries can become narrowed by fatty cholesterol deposits and as a result, the blood flow through the arteries can become restricted, perhaps leading to a clot causing either a stroke or heart attack.

In addition to eating less fat, it is probably wise to limit one's consumption of foods which are high in dietary cholesterol simply because we do not need it. These include egg yolks, kidneys and other offal, certain shellfish, and to a small extent, all animal products.

3. Eat Less Fat

Contrary to the former belief that dietary cholesterol is primarily responsible for increasing blood cholesterol levels, we know now that a high-fat diet can be far more damaging to one's heart than one which is high in dietary cholesterol. So, reducing your fat intake is the most effective way of lowering your blood cholesterol level.

Having said that, fat is a necessary part of our diets as it provides an important source of food energy. There are, however, different types of fat and in order to tell the 'good' from the 'bad', it will help to understand a little more about them.

The 3 basic types of fat are saturates, monounsaturates and polyunsaturates.

SATURATED fats are those which contribute to increased blood cholesterol levels and should be avoided as far as possible. They are found mainly in dairy products and animal fats such as butter, cream, whole milk, cheese, lard, dripping and suet. They are also found in coconut and palm oils as well as in those margarines not specified as polyunsaturated or monounsaturated. Generally speaking, any fat which becomes hard on refrigeration is classified as saturated, and most processed foods such as crisps, chocolate and biscuits contain saturated fats.

MONOUNSATURATED fats are thought to have a lowering effect on blood cholesterol levels and are found in olives, rapeseed, avocados, most nuts, and oily fish such as herring, salmon and mackerel.

POLYUNSATURATED fats circulate in the blood and can help to lower blood cholesterol levels. They are necessary as they contain essential fatty acids that our bodies cannot manufacture. Polyunsaturated fats are found in vegetable and seed oils, particularly safflower, sunflower, corn and soyabean oils.

Remember that even 'good' fats contain some saturated fatty acids and that as all fats are extremely high in Calories (containing more than twice that of carbohydrates and proteins), Weight Watchers aim is to reduce overall fat intake to a minimum. Try using low-fat dairy alternatives and buy only lean meats. Remember to trim any visible fat from meat before it is cooked and always remove the skin from poultry.

4. Maintain a Healthy Weight

As 1 in 6 women and 1 in 8 men in Britain are clinically obese, it is not surprising that we have such a high rate of heart-related disease and death in this country.

Obesity and heart disease are directly related in that the more overweight you are, the harder your heart must work. In addition, most overweight people tend to consume a lot of fat and get little exercise, both of which increase your risks of developing heart disease. This is not to suggest that thin people cannot suffer from high blood cholesterol levels or heart problems, simply that obesity adds yet another level of risk.

Moreover, being overweight can be just plain miserable. Clothes feel tight, waistbands pinch and there is a constant battle to avoid facing oneself in the mirror. Low self-esteem is a common factor among people who feel they are overweight, and self-confidence certainly soars with the successful loss of just a few pounds.

Being seriously overweight as a teenager, and then again as a young mum, I know at first hand about the painful teasing at school and the terror of drawing attention to myself in case anyone should ask me how much I weighed or what size clothes I wore. As my weight problem was very definitely linked to bad eating habits and a lack of understanding about food, the best thing I ever did was to switch from a diet which was far too high in fats and protein, to one high in fibre and carbohydrates. Both Weight Watchers and the British Heart Foundation maintain that the only way to lose weight permanently is to change your eating habits for life. By losing weight and eating sensibly you can reduce your risk of developing heart disease.

5. Exercise More

Exercise has so many benefits to our hearts and overall sense of well-being that it seems crazy we don't spend more time doing it! Not only does it help to burn off fat and increase weight loss, but it can strengthen the heart and lungs, tone muscles, increase flexibility, and generally improve mobility and stamina. Exercise is also a great way to relieve stress, improving one's emotional and mental well-being, both of which are important in maintaining a healthy heart. Whether you want to join a fitness club, go dancing with friends, or simply walk briskly to and from work instead of driving every day, make a point of exercising for at least 20 minutes, 3 times a week.

6. Reduce Your Stress

Stress can be physically unhealthy as well as being emotionally and mentally draining. When one is under stress, adrenaline is released into the blood stream, one's blood pressure rises and the heart is forced to work harder.

Exercise is an effective means of controlling stress – who doesn't feel better after a walk in the fresh air or a whirl around the dance floor? You should also make time to relax and to face your problems – stress doesn't go away just because you're too busy to deal with it. Most importantly, don't keep your worries to yourself. Talking to others can greatly reduce your stress and help you to cope with things – just think of how helpful Weight Watchers Meetings can be.

7. Lessen Your Alcohol Consumption

Alcohol, like sugar, contains 'empty' Calories which have no nutritional value, so it's in your best interests to refrain from too many gin and tonics. However, a moderate amount of alcohol is actually thought to be beneficial to the heart, so, as long as you can stick to a single glass of wine and fit it into your Programme Selections, feel free to enjoy a tipple! In fact, in the Mediterranean, where even quite young children are given wine (mixed with water), instances of heart disease remain relatively low. This has as much to do with their traditional diet, which is high in fruits, vegetables, fish and olive oil, and low in animal fats.

8. Increase the Fibre in Your Diet

If fat is the heart's worst enemy, then fibre is definitely the Weight Watcher Member's best friend. Filling and sustaining, most fibre-rich foods contain fewer Calories than fat and protein–rich ones.

There are 2 types of fibre; soluble and insoluble. SOLUBLE FIBRE is useful in lowering blood sugar and cholesterol levels. One of the best known sources of soluble fibre is found in oats and oat products so you can enjoy a daily bowl of porridge with a little skimmed milk and sweetener. (It's also delicious with dried fruits such as apricots, figs or dates which will provide you with even more fibre.) Other good sources of soluble fibre include pulses – dried or canned – which are great in salads, soups and casseroles; pectin–rich fruits such as apples, strawberries and citrus fruits; and most types of vegetables.

INSOLUBLE DIETARY FIBRE passes through the system without being absorbed and prevents constipation and other bowel disorders including cancer. Wheat bran is probably the best source of insoluble fibre and is readily available in wholewheat products such as bread and cereals. Fruits and vegetables also provide insoluble fibre – but try to eat the skins wherever possible as well as the seeds of such fruits as figs, tomatoes and kiwis.

You will find that many of the recipes in this book are fibre-rich. As a general rule, fill your plate with vegetables, add pulses to your soups, and snack on fresh or dried fruits. When you're craving a starchy snack, have a thick slice of wholewheat toast topped with Marmite and a sliced tomato. This should satisfy your craving as well as pleasing your heart!

Increasing your dietary fibre will take some adjustment by your body so it's best to do so gradually and to drink plenty of water to help flush the fibre through your system. You may find flatulence (wind) a bit of a problem at first, but don't worry, your digestive system will quickly adjust, and any wind or bloated feeling will soon ease.

9. Cut Back on Salt

Cutting back on salt will benefit your heart in several ways. Not only will it help to reduce your blood pressure, but reducing your salt intake really does help to prevent water retention, particularly during menstruation. Some people find that headaches and 'nerviness' are also eased by beating the salt habit. If you take the salt cellar off the kitchen table and gradually stop using salt when you cook vegetables, you'll find that you soon get used to less salt and begin to enjoy the natural flavours of foods. Even better, as you lose your taste for salty foods, you'll lessen your cravings for crisps and other commercially prepared foods which tend to be very high in sodium (as well as fat).

10. Change Your Cooking Methods

If you're cutting back on fats and proteins and increasing your intake of carbohydrates and fibre-rich foods, you'll probably find your cooking methods are changing without much thought or effort on your part. However, it is worth thinking about HOW you cook as well as WHAT you cook.

Choose methods which don't call for additional fat. Grill, roast, steam, poach or microwave your food instead of frying it. If you must fry your food, sauté or stir-fry using a non-stick pan or wok so that you use a minimum of fat. Take advantage of sunny days and barbecue your supper – the smoky flavours produced will more than make up for the lack of oil. Better yet, get into the habit of eating vegetables raw, and reap the benefits of the extra vitamins and minerals you will consume. Experiment with fresh herbs and begin to enjoy the real taste of good foods, knowing that you'll feel and look great at the end of the day!

Soups and Light Meals

The recipes in this section are just right for light lunches or as a first course when you're entertaining. Good results are hard to come by with tired, wilted vegetables, so always use top-quality, fresh ingredients for the best taste, value and appearance.

You will love the fresh citrus tang in the Tomato, Celery and Orange Soup (page 10), and the creamy Lentil and Yogurt Soup (page 10) is sure to become a family favourite. A bowl of warming soup is always welcome and surprisingly filling when served with a wholemeal roll. Don't be tempted to butter your bread or even use a low-fat spread – try it 'au naturel' as the continentals do – the flavour of fresh wholemeal bread is simply wonderful all on its own.

For a healthy but delicious party treat, serve the Blue Cheese Dip with Vegetable Sticks (page 16) or the Salmon Paté (page 16). Both are rich in taste yet low in saturated fats, and are sure to keep your guests coming back for more.

Mexican Salad

Like a salad ordered in a Mexican restaurant, this colourful combination of ingredients is bright and appealing. Low in fat and with plenty of fibre, this somewhat different salad dish tastes sensational and looks great on the table.

Serves: 4
Preparation time: 15 minutes
Freezing: not recommended
Selections per serving: ½ Fruit; 1½ Protein; 1½ Vegetable; 25 Optional Calories
Calories per serving: 220

(V) if using vegetarian Cheddar cheese

8 oz (240 g) mixed salad leaves (e.g. Oak Leaf, radicchio, Little Gem, etc.), rinsed and drained
6-inch (15 cm) piece of cucumber, chopped
1 large carrot, grated
2 tomatoes, chopped
1 small green pepper, de-seeded and sliced
3 oz (90 g) canned red kidney beans, drained and rinsed
2 oz (60 g) raisins
2 teaspoons lime juice
5 fl oz (150 ml) natural fromage frais (up to 8% fat)
1 teaspoon tomato purée
1 teaspoon coarse grain mustard
4 oz (120 g) half-fat Cheddar cheese, grated
salt and freshly ground black pepper

1. Arrange the salad leaves on four serving plates and top with the cucumber, carrot, tomatoes, green pepper, red kidney beans and raisins. Sprinkle with the lime juice.
2. Blend the fromage frais with the tomato purée and mustard. Season lightly with salt and pepper and spoon over the salads.
3. Divide the grated cheese between each plate and serve immediately.

Tomato, Celery and Orange Soup

A warming soup that's bursting with flavour, serve it with wholemeal bread or rolls, warmed in the oven for a few minutes. Remember to add the Carbohydrate Selections!

Serves: 4
Preparation time: 20 minutes
Cooking time: 30 minutes
Freezing: recommended for up to 3 months
Selections per serving: 1/2 Fat; 3 Vegetable; 35 Optional Calories
Calories per serving: 110

(V)

1 tablespoon olive oil
1 onion, chopped
4 oz (120 g) potato, peeled and diced
1 garlic clove, crushed
1 celery stick, chopped
1 large carrot, diced
1 1/2 lb (720 g) ripe tomatoes, cut in quarters
1 tablespoon tomato purée
juice of 1/2 medium-size orange
3/4 pint (450 ml) vegetable stock
1 teaspoon dried basil
salt and freshly ground black pepper
thin strips of blanched orange rind, to garnish

1. Heat the oil in a large saucepan and add the onion, potato, garlic, celery and carrot. Cook, stirring frequently, for 5 minutes or until the vegetables are softened.
2. Add the tomatoes and cook for 2–3 minutes more, stirring constantly.
3. Add the tomato purée, orange juice, vegetable stock and basil. Bring to a boil and then reduce the heat, cover and simmer for 25 minutes, or until the vegetables are tender.
4. Pass the soup through a sieve to extract skins and pips. Check the seasoning before reheating gently. Serve garnished with the blanched orange rind.

Cook's note: to blanch the orange rind,cover thin strips of peel with boiling water. Leave for 2–3 minutes and then drain through a sieve. The same can be done with other citrus fruits such as lemons, limes or grapefruit.

Lentil and Yogurt Soup

Coriander goes well with lentils and gives this savoury soup an exotic Eastern flavour.

Serves: 6
Preparation time: 10 minutes
Cooking time: 50 minutes
Freezing: recommended (without yogurt) for up to 3 months
Selections per serving: 1 Carbohydrate; 1/2 Protein; 1 Vegetable; 35 Optional Calories
Calories per serving: 165

2 teaspoons corn or olive oil
2 oz (60 g) lean back bacon, trimmed of any fat and chopped
1 onion, chopped
1 carrot, diced
6 oz (180 g) mushrooms, wiped and chopped
6 oz (180 g) orange lentils, rinsed and drained
2 pints (1.2 litres) chicken stock
1 1/2 teaspoons ground coriander
6 tablespoons low-fat natural yogurt
salt and freshly ground black pepper
1 tablespoon snipped fresh chives, to serve

Lentil and Yogurt Soup
Tomato, Celery and Orange Soup

❶ Heat the oil in a large saucepan and sauté the bacon with the onion and carrot for 5 minutes, until the onion is translucent.

❷ Add the mushrooms, lentils and chicken stock. Season with the coriander, a little salt and pepper and bring to a boil. Reduce the heat and simmer gently for 40 minutes, or until the lentils are soft.

❸ Stir in the yogurt and reheat gently. Ladle into warm soup bowls, sprinkle with the snipped chives and serve immediately.

Vegetarian option: omit the bacon and use vegetable stock. This will remove the Protein Selection and reduce the Optional Calories to 25 per serving. The Calories per serving will be 150.

Melon with Prawns and Strawberries

Although prawns are fairly high in cholesterol, it's okay to indulge in them once in a while. Enjoy this delicious starter when you next have friends to supper.

Serves: 4
Preparation time: 20 minutes
Freezing: not recommended
Selections per serving: 1½ Fat; 1 Fruit; 1 Protein; 1 Vegetable; 25 Optional Calories
Calories per serving: 145

½ medium-size avocado
½ teaspoon lemon juice
1 medium-size, ripe seasonal melon (i.e. ogen, cantaloupe or honeydew)
1 celery heart, chopped
4 oz (120 g) strawberries, hulled and sliced
8 oz (240 g) cooked, peeled prawns (thawed if frozen)
2 Little Gem lettuces, rinsed and torn into pieces

For the dressing:
8 oz (240 g) strawberries
1 teaspoon caster sugar
2 teaspoons olive oil
1 tablespoon unsweetened orange juice
2 teaspoons chopped fresh parsley
salt and freshly ground black pepper

❶ Peel and chop the avocado and place it in a mixing bowl. Sprinkle it with the lemon juice to prevent it from discolouring.

❷ Halve the melon, discard the seeds and scoop out the flesh using a melon baller (or cut it into cubes). Gently combine the melon, chopped celery, strawberries and prawns with the avocado and refrigerate until needed.

❸ Meanwhile, purée the dressing ingredients in a food processor or liquidiser.

❹ Arrange the lettuce on 4 plates and divide the prawn mixture between them. Pour the dressing over and serve immediately.

Cook's notes: when melons are ripe they should 'give' slightly when pressed at the stalk end.

Wrap up melons well if storing them in the refrigerator as otherwise they will permeate everything around them with their heady scent.

Chicken Soup

Serves: 4
Preparation time: 15 minutes
Cooking time: 30 minutes
Freezing: recommended for up to 3 months
Selections per serving: 1/2 Carbohydrate; 1/4 Milk; 1 1/2 Protein; 1 1/2 Vegetable; 25 Optional Calories
Calories per serving: 190

1 garlic clove, crushed
1 onion, chopped finely
1 tablespoon chopped fresh tarragon
10 oz (300 g) potato, peeled and chopped finely
1 small celery stick, chopped finely
1 carrot, chopped finely
1 pint (600 ml) chicken stock
2 oz (60 g) low-fat soft cheese
1/2 pint (300 ml) skimmed milk
6 oz (180 g) cooked chicken, chopped
freshly ground black pepper
chopped fresh parsley, to garnish

1. Place the garlic, onion, tarragon, potato, celery and carrot in a large saucepan. Pour in the stock, bring to a boil, cover and simmer for 25 minutes, or until the vegetables are tender.
2. Transfer the soup to a liquidiser or food processor and blend until smooth. Return to a clean saucepan and add the soft cheese a little at a time, stirring until melted.
3. Stir in the milk and bring back to the boil, stirring constantly. Simmer for 2 minutes more.
4. Add the cooked chicken, season to taste with black pepper and reheat gently, stirring constantly until piping hot.
5. Ladle the soup into warm bowls and sprinkle each with a little chopped parsley. Serve immediately.

Curried Mushrooms

This tangy starter will appeal to anyone who enjoys Indian food.

Serves: 4
Preparation time: 15 minutes
Freezing: not recommended
Selections per serving: 1 1/2 Vegetable; 35 Optional Calories
Calories per serving: 65

1 teaspoon medium curry powder
1 tablespoon reduced-fat mayonnaise
4 tablespoons low-fat natural yogurt
1 tablespoon unsweetened orange juice
2 teaspoons mango chutney
12 oz (360 g) small button mushrooms, wiped and halved
1/2 Iceburg lettuce, shredded
2-inch (5 cm) piece of cucumber, chopped
salt

(V)

1. Combine the curry powder and mayonnaise in a large mixing bowl. Add the yogurt, orange juice and chutney and stir. Season with a little salt.
2. Add the mushrooms and toss to coat them thoroughly with the dressing. Cover and refrigerate.
3. Arrange the lettuce and cucumber on four serving plates and top evenly with the curry mixture. Serve immediately.

Curried Mushrooms
Chicken Soup

Blue Cheese Dip with Vegetable Sticks

As vegetables are virtually unlimited on the Weight Watchers Programme, you can serve your favourites with this creamy dip.

Serves: 4
Preparation time: 10 minutes + 1 hour chilling
Freezing: not recommended
Selections per serving: 1/4 Milk; 1/2 Protein; 1/2 Vegetable; 25 Optional Calories
Calories per serving: 65

2 tablespoons reduced-fat mayonnaise
5 fl oz (150 ml) low-fat natural yogurt
2 oz (60 g) blue Stilton cheese, crumbled
2 carrots, cut in large sticks
1 red pepper, de-seeded and cut in strips
2 celery stalks, cut in large sticks

(V) if using vegetarian blue cheese

1. Blend the mayonnaise, yogurt and blue cheese together in a large mixing bowl.
2. Transfer the mixture to a serving bowl and refrigerate for at least 1 hour or until ready to serve.
3. Arrange the vegetables on a plate and serve with the chilled dip.

Salmon Paté

No one will realise that you have used canned salmon to make this delicious paté. Pretty to serve and full of flavour, it's ideal for a summer evening.

Serves: 4
Preparation time: 10 minutes + 2 hours chilling
Freezing: not recommended
Selections per serving: 2 Protein; 20 Optional Calories
Calories per serving: 145

7 oz (210 g) canned salmon, drained
2 garlic cloves, crushed (optional)
4 oz (120 g) low-fat soft cheese
2 tablespoons low-fat natural yogurt
1 teaspoon lemon juice
2 teaspoons tomato purée
salt and freshly ground black pepper
lemon slices, to garnish

1. Put the salmon, garlic (if using), soft cheese, yogurt, lemon juice and tomato purée into a liquidiser or food processor. Blend until smooth and season to taste with a little salt and pepper.
2. Pour the mixture into a serving bowl, cover and refrigerate for 2 hours before serving, garnished with lemon slices.

Cook's note: most patés are best made at least 30 minutes before serving to allow the flavours to develop.

Blue Cheese Dip with Vegetable Sticks
Salmon Paté

Salads and Vegetable Dishes

Cooking should be pleasurable and you'll find the recipes in this section appealing, delicious and simple to prepare.

Colourful, high-fibre vegetables should be central to any heart-conscious eating programme. Bursting with vitamins, minerals and flavour, yet containing only traces of fat, vegetables are the ideal food for cooking Weight Watchers style.

It's worth noting that lettuce, cucumber, watercress etc. are largely made up of water and contain little food value and few Calories, so salads do need other vegetables, nuts, pulses and dried fruits to add extra fibre, texture, colour and nutrients to your meals.

Another caution is regarding salad dressings, which can easily add Calories and fat to an otherwise heart-healthy dish. Avoid commercially prepared dressings unless they are labelled as fat-free. Dressings made at home with lemon or tomato juice, fresh herbs, a little seasoning and a tiny amount of oil are quick to prepare and are by far the healthier choice. The dressings in the following recipes are low in fat and high on flavour and my guess is that once you've tasted them you'll prefer the lighter option.

Make a habit of including at least one salad or vegetable dish in all of your meals, whether as an accompaniment or as the main course. The Swede and Parsnip Purée (page 23) makes a delicious lunch when served with a salad of fresh tomatoes and basil, or try the Fruity Curried Coleslaw (below) with barbecued chicken or fish for a tasty summertime supper.

Fruity Curried Coleslaw

With its festive colours, this tangy salad is perfect to serve during the Christmas season. The fresh orange juice enhances the curry flavour and makes it a great accompaniment to poultry or egg dishes.

Serves: 4
Preparation time: 15 minutes
Freezing: not recommended
Selections per serving: 1 Fruit; 1/4 Milk; 1 1/2 Vegetable; 10 Optional Calories
Calories per serving: 130

(V)

6 oz (180 g) red cabbage, shredded
6 oz (180 g) white cabbage, shredded
1 medium-size dessert apple, cored and chopped
4 oz (120 g) celery, chopped finely
1/2 small red onion, chopped
3 oz (90 g) dried, stoned dates, chopped
5 fl oz (150 ml) low-fat natural yogurt
zest and juice of 1/2 medium-size orange
1 teaspoon medium curry powder
salt

1. Mix together the red and white cabbage in a salad bowl. Add the apple, celery, onion and dates.
2. Blend the yogurt, orange zest and juice and curry powder together in a small bowl and season to taste with a little salt.
3. Pour the dressing over the cabbage mixture and toss to coat the salad thoroughly. Cover and refrigerate until ready to serve.

Fruity Curried Coleslaw

Bean Sprout Salad with Oriental Dressing

Enjoy this tasty salad as an easy lunch or light supper. Served with potatoes boiled in their skins or warmed wholemeal bread, everyone will enjoy the sweetness of the grapes combined with the chicken and the spicy Oriental dressing. This will be a sure hit with teenagers, and indeed anyone who enjoys Chinese food.

Serves: 4
Preparation time: 15 minutes
Cooking time: 10 minutes
Freezing: not recommended
Selections per serving: 1/2 Carbohydrate; 1 Fat; 1 1/2 Protein; 1 Vegetable; 25 Optional Calories
Calories per serving: 170

1 oz (30 g) flaked almonds
6 oz (180 g) frozen sweetcorn
4 oz (120 g) Iceberg lettuce, shredded
1 head of chicory, shredded
4 oz (120 g) bean sprouts
1/2 red pepper, de-seeded and chopped
3-inch (8 cm) piece of cucumber, chopped
2 oz (60 g) black seedless grapes, halved
6 oz (180 g) cooked chicken breast, chopped
2 teaspoons sesame or sunflower oil
2 teaspoons red wine vinegar
1 teaspoon medium sherry
1 teaspoon light soy sauce
1 garlic clove, crushed

❶ Scatter the flaked almonds on a baking sheet and grill them until golden, stirring them occasionally to toast evenly. Take care not to burn them as they brown very quickly.

❷ Put the sweetcorn in a suitable container, cover and microwave on 100% (full power) for 3 minutes. Alternatively, cook it in boiling water for 5 minutes, stir and drain. Turn out the sweetcorn into a sieve and rinse with cold water to cool it quickly. Drain thoroughly and transfer it to a serving bowl.

❸ Add the lettuce, chicory, bean sprouts, red pepper, cucumber, grapes and chicken breast to the corn.

❹ Combine the oil, red wine vinegar, sherry, soy sauce and garlic in a screw top jar. Shake well to mix. Pour over the salad and toss until well coated.

❺ Top the salad with the toasted almonds and serve immediately.

Bean Sprout Salad with Oriental Dressing

Festive Rice Ring

Serve this colourful salad on a bed of fresh salad leaves at your next buffet party.

Serves: 4
Preparation time: 15 minutes
Cooking time: 35 minutes + minimum 1 hour chilling
Freezing: not recommended
Selections per serving: 2 Carbohydrate; 1/2 Fat; 1/2 Protein; 1 1/2 Vegetable; 25 Optional Calories
Calories per serving: 335

8 oz (240 g) brown rice
3 tomatoes, peeled, chopped and de-seeded
2 spring onions, chopped
1/2 small red pepper, chopped
2 tablespoons chopped fresh parsley
4 oz (120 g) black seedless grapes, halved
2 oz (60 g) Edam cheese, grated
10 oz (300 g) canned chopped mushrooms, drained
1 tablespoon olive oil
salt and freshly ground black pepper
salad leaves, to serve

(V)

❶ Boil the rice in a large covered saucepan of lightly salted water for 35 minutes, or until the rice is tender.
❷ Tip the rice into a colander and rinse with cold, running water to cool it quickly. Drain thoroughly and transfer it to a mixing bowl.
❸ Combine the tomatoes, spring onions, red pepper, parsley, grapes, grated cheese and mushrooms with the rice mixture.
❹ Use a little of the olive oil to lightly grease an 8-inch (20 cm) ring mould. Add the remaining oil to the rice mixture and season to taste with salt and pepper.
❺ Toss to coat the rice thoroughly and then turn it into the ring mould. Pack it down tightly with the back of a spoon and refrigerate for at least 1 hour or until ready to serve.
❻ Turn the rice ring out on to a serving dish, garnish with salad leaves and serve at once.

Cook's note: this rice ring can be prepared a day in advance and refrigerated in the ring mould until ready to serve.

To turn the ring out, place a serving plate over the ring and quickly turn it over, as you would a jelly. Should the ring collapse, simply transfer it to a serving dish and fluff it through with a fork.

Spicy Glazed Vegetables

A colourful vegetable dish with a hint of the Orient, this is delicious with eggs or chicken and is also good to serve with the Sunday roast. Make sure you serve the vegetables tender yet crisp, so that they retain some 'bite'.

Serves: 4
Preparation time: 20 minutes
Cooking time: 12 minutes
Freezing: not recommended
Selections per serving: ½ Carbohydrate; ½ Fat; 2½ Vegetable; 45 Optional Calories
Calories per serving: 100

(V)

6 oz (180 g) carrots, cut in matchsticks
a bunch of spring onions, chopped
8 oz (240 g) broccoli spears
9 oz (270 g) baby courgettes, halved
9 oz (270 g) babycorn cobs
3 oz (90 g) bean sprouts
3 tablespoons dry white wine
1 oz (30 g) low-fat spread
1 teaspoon clear honey
2 teaspoons light soy sauce
½ teaspoon cinnamon
½ teaspoon paprika
1 tablespoon chopped fresh parsley or 1 teaspoon dried parsley

1. Steam the vegetables for 8–10 minutes until tender. Alternatively, simmer them in ½ pint (300 ml) of boiling water in a covered saucepan, until just tender, and drain, discarding the liquid.
2. Combine the wine, low-fat spread, honey, soy sauce, cinnamon, paprika and parsley in a medium-size saucepan.
3. Add the cooked vegetables and bring to a boil, stirring constantly.
4. Serve the vegetables with their spicy cooking juices poured over them.

Swede and Parsnip Purée

Serves: 4
Preparation time: 15 minutes
Cooking time: 35 minutes
Freezing: not recommended
Selections per serving: ½ Carbohydrate; 1½ Protein; 3 Vegetable; 15 Optional Calories
Calories per serving: 220

(V) if using vegetarian cheese

2½ lb (1.1 kg) swede, peeled and chopped finely
1 vegetable stock cube (optional)
8 oz (240 g) parsnips, peeled and sliced
grated zest and juice of 1 medium-size orange
2 tablespoons chopped fresh mixed herbs or 2 teaspoons dried mixed herbs
6 oz (180 g) goats cheese, crumbled or 6 oz (180 g) feta cheese
salt and freshly ground black pepper
sprigs of fresh parsley or coriander, to garnish

1. Place the swede in a saucepan and cover with either cold salted water or cold water plus the stock cube, if using. Bring to a boil and then lower the heat, cover and simmer for 15 minutes.
2. Add the parsnips and simmer for 15 minutes more, or until the vegetables are tender. Drain the vegetables and return them to the pan, keeping it off the heat.
3. Mash the swede and parsnips with the orange zest, juice and mixed herbs. Season to taste with a little salt and pepper. Return to the heat for several minutes, stirring constantly, until heated through and any excess moisture has evaporated.
5. Remove from the heat and gradually stir in the cheese. Transfer to a warm dish, garnish with the parsley or coriander and serve at once.

Mixed Bean Salad with Cottage Cheese

The cottage cheese with chives not only makes this a pretty dish, but provides a valuable source of protein with little or no extra fat.

Serves: 4
Preparation time: 15 minutes + 10 minutes standing
Cooking time: 8 minutes
Freezing: not recommended
Selections per serving: 1/2 Carbohydrate; 1/2 Fat; 1/2 Fruit; 1 1/2 Protein; 1 Vegetable; 35 Optional Calories
Calories per serving: 225

6 oz (180 g) dwarf green beans, sliced
2 tablespoons white wine vinegar
1 tablespoon olive oil
2 teaspoons coarse grain mustard
10 oz (300 g) canned red kidney beans, drained
1/2 red pepper, de-seeded and chopped
1 medium-size dessert apple, cored and chopped
1 celery stalk, chopped
2 spring onions, chopped
1 oz (30 g) sultanas
12 oz (360 g) low-fat cottage cheese with chives, to serve
salt and freshly ground black pepper

1. Cook the dwarf beans in a small amount of boiling water for 6–8 minutes, or until just tender. Drain and rinse with cold running water to cool quickly. Alternatively, place the beans on a microwave-proof dish and sprinkle with 2 tablespoons of water. Cover and microwave on 100% (full power) for 5–6 minutes, stirring once during cooking. Allow to stand for 2 minutes.
2. Combine the vinegar, olive oil and mustard in a screw-top jar. Season with a little salt and pepper and shake well to mix.
3. Gently combine the green beans, kidney beans, red pepper, apple, celery, spring onions and sultanas in a large mixing bowl. Pour the dressing over and toss to coat thoroughly. Set aside for 10 minutes to allow the flavours to blend.
4. Divide the salad between four serving plates, top each with 3 oz (90 g) of cottage cheese and serve immediately.

Spicy Glazed Vegetables
Mixed Bean Salad with Cottage Cheese

Main Meals

By choosing regularly from a wide variety of foods not only will you feel good, but you'll avoid the boredom which stems from 'diet monotony' and not be tempted to eat high-fat and sugary snacks.

The recipes in this chapter use a broad selection of ingredients and are designed to appeal to all of the senses – texture, smell, taste and, of course, common sense! You'll find vegetables, pulses, meat, fish and dairy products in balanced proportions with an emphasis on simple preparation and great taste.

Your family will love Pasta Ratatouille (page 32), a filling, nutty, wholewheat spaghetti dish topped with vegetables and sprinkled with grated cheese. The Chicken Pittas (page 30) are terrific for a party, and how about Pork with Black-eyed Beans and Apricots (page 38) for a delicious midweek supper that takes only 15 minutes to prepare! Whatever you choose, remember that not only will your friends and family love it – your heart will thank you for it too!

Cod and Courgette Kebabs with Pineapple

This delicious fish dish can be prepared in advance and then cooked at the last minute. Serve it with a salad and new potatoes, baked in their jackets.

Serves: 4
Preparation time: 15 minutes + 1 hour chilling
Cooking time: 8 minutes
Freezing: not recommended
Selections per serving: 1/2 Fat; 1 1/2 Protein; 1 Vegetable; 20 Optional Calories
Calories per serving: 135

1 lb (480 g) cod fillet, skinned and cubed
8 button mushrooms
1 tablespoon olive oil
1 garlic clove, crushed
juice and finely grated zest of 1/2 lemon
1/2 teaspoon anchovy essence (optional)
1 teaspoon mixed dried herbs
1 courgette, cut in 8 slices
1 small red pepper, de-seeded and cut in 1-inch (2.5 cm) pieces
2 canned pineapple rings (2 oz/60 g), drained and cut in 1-inch (2.5 cm) chunks

1. Place the cubes of cod and the mushrooms in a shallow dish.
2. Mix together the olive oil, garlic, lemon juice and zest, anchovy essence (if using) and the mixed herbs. Spoon over the fish and mushrooms. Cover and refrigerate for about 1 hour.
3. Preheat the grill to medium-hot.
4. Carefully thread the cod and mushrooms on to 4 kebab skewers, alternating them with the courgette, red pepper and pineapple chunks.
5. Brush each threaded kebab with a little of the lemon and oil marinade and place on the grill rack.
6. Grill for 6–8 minutes, turning occasionally, or until the kebabs are cooked through. Serve at once.

Egg and Leek Mornay
Cod and Courgette Kebabs with Pineapple

Egg and Leek Mornay

With their wonderful mild onion flavour, leeks combine well with bacon and cheese. This dish smells so appetising as it bakes that it will soon become a family favourite.

Serves: 4
Preparation time: 20 minutes
Cooking time: 30 minutes
Freezing: not recommended
Selections per serving: 1/2 Carbohydrate; 1/2 Fat; 1/4 Milk; 3 Protein; 1 Vegetable; 55 Optional Calories
Calories per serving: 320

12 oz (360 g) leeks, cleaned and sliced
3 oz (90 g) lean back bacon, trimmed of any fat
4 eggs, hard-boiled and halved
3/4 pint (450 ml) skimmed milk
1 oz (30 g) wholemeal flour
1 tablespoon soft polyunsaturated margarine
1 teaspoon ready-prepared English mustard
3 oz (90 g) half-fat Cheddar cheese, grated
2 oz (60 g) wholemeal breadcrumbs
salt and freshly ground black pepper

1. Preheat the oven to Gas Mark 5/190°C/375°F. Preheat the grill to medium-hot.
2. Cook the leeks in a small amount of lightly salted boiling water until just tender – this should take about 5 minutes. Drain and transfer them to a large ovenproof dish.
3. Meanwhile, grill the bacon until crisp. Chop the bacon roughly and sprinkle it over the leeks.
4. Arrange the hard-boiled eggs evenly over the bed of leeks.
5. Combine the milk, flour and margarine in a small saucepan. Heat, stirring constantly with a wire whisk, until thickened and smooth. Remove from the heat and stir in the mustard and 2 oz (60 g) of the grated cheese, allowing it to melt slowly in the heat of the sauce.
6. Season the sauce with a little salt and freshly ground black pepper and pour it over the eggs and leeks to coat them thoroughly.
7. Mix the remaining cheese and breadcrumbs together and sprinkle them evenly over the eggs and leeks. Bake for approximately 20 minutes or until golden brown.

Cook's tip: always cool hard-boiled eggs under cold running water directly after cooking to prevent them from developing a grey ring between the yolk and the white.

Vegetable Lasagne

No one will miss the meat in this filling pasta dish. Serve it with crusty wholemeal bread to soak up the juices, but don't forget to add the Carbohydrate Selections.

Serves: 4
Preparation time: 20 minutes
Cooking time: 1 hour
Freezing: recommended for up to 2 months
Selections per serving: 1 Carbohydrate; 1 Fat; 1/2 Milk; 1 Protein; 3 1/2 Vegetable; 45 Optional Calories
Calories per serving: 415

2 teaspoons olive oil
1 large celery stalk, chopped finely
1 large carrot, diced
1 onion, chopped
10 oz (300 g) broccoli spears
6 oz (180 g) mushrooms, chopped
14 oz (420 g) canned plum tomatoes in their juice
2 tablespoons tomato purée
1 garlic clove, crushed
3 fl oz (90 ml) dry cider
1 teaspoon dried oregano
4 oz (120 g) no pre-cook lasagne verde sheets
salt and freshly ground black pepper

For the cheese sauce:

3 teaspoons soft polyunsaturated margarine
1 1/2 oz (45 g) wholemeal flour
1 pint (600 ml) skimmed milk
1 teaspoon prepared English mustard
1 oz (30 g) parmesan cheese, grated
3 oz (90 g) half-fat Cheddar cheese, grated

❶ Heat the olive oil in a pan and cook the celery, carrot and onion for 5 minutes, stirring, until softened.

❷ Stir in the broccoli, mushrooms, tomatoes, tomato purée, garlic, cider and oregano. Season with salt and pepper and bring to a boil. Reduce the heat, cover the pan and simmer for 20 minutes.

❸ Meanwhile, prepare the cheese sauce. Heat the margarine, flour and milk in a saucepan, stirring constantly with a wire whisk until thickened, smooth and heated through. Remove from the heat, stir in the mustard and season to taste with a little salt and pepper. Stir in half of the grated cheese, to melt.

❹ Preheat the oven to Gas Mark 5/190°C/375°F.

❺ Spoon half of the vegetable mixture into a shallow ovenproof dish and layer with half of the lasagne sheets followed by half of the cheese sauce. Repeat the layers in the same order, finishing with a layer of cheese sauce.

❻ Sprinkle with the remaining cheese and bake for 35–40 minutes, until bubbling and golden.

Cook's tip: you can prepare the lasagne well ahead and refrigerate it until ready to bake. This will enhance the flavours and make the dish even more scrumptious!

Chicken Risotto

Risotto is especially delicious when made with nutty brown rice. This recipe is full of flavour and very filling, so just serve it with a tossed green salad (making sure you use a low-fat dressing)!

Serves: 4
Preparation time: 15 minutes
Cooking time: 40 minutes
Freezing: recommended for up to 3 months
Selections per serving: 2 Carbohydrate; 1½ Fat; 2 Protein; 1½ Vegetable, 15 Optional Calories
Calories per serving: 370

2 tablespoons olive oil
1 large onion, chopped
1 carrot, chopped finely
2 garlic cloves, crushed
1 green pepper, de-seeded and chopped
8 oz (240 g) easy-cook brown rice
4 tablespoons dry cider
1¼ pints (750 ml) chicken stock
4 small courgettes, sliced
3 tablespoons chopped fresh parsley
8 oz (240 g) skinless, boneless chicken breast, cooked and chopped
1 tablespoon grated parmesan cheese
freshly ground black pepper
a few sprigs of parsley, to garnish

❶ Heat the oil in a large saucepan and sauté the onion and carrot for 5 minutes, until softened.
❷ Stir in the garlic, green pepper and rice and then add the cider and chicken stock. Season with a little freshly ground black pepper. Bring to a boil, cover and simmer for 25 minutes.
❸ Add the courgettes and cook for 8 minutes more. Remove the lid and, if the risotto seems rather wet, boil it for 2–3 minutes, stirring constantly. Otherwise, stir in the parsley and chicken and cook for 2–3 minutes more.
❹ Sprinkle with the parmesan cheese and serve immediately, garnished with the sprigs of parsley.

Chicken Pittas

Pitta pockets are always popular and this recipe would make a great patio meal or picnic dish.

Serves: 4
Preparation time: 15 minutes + 30 minutes marinating
Cooking time: 15 minutes
Freezing: not recommended
Selections per serving: 1 Carbohydrate; ¼ Milk; 3 Protein; 1 Vegetable
Calories per serving: 250

15 oz (450 g) skinless, boneless chicken breasts
5 fl oz (150 ml) low-fat natural yogurt
2 teaspoons lemon juice
2 teaspoons paprika
½ teaspoon hot chilli powder
2 teaspoons tomato purée
1 garlic clove, crushed
4 x 1 oz (30 g) wholemeal pitta breads
½ small Iceburg lettuce, shredded
1 small onion, sliced thinly
3-inch (8 cm) piece of cucumber, chopped
salt and freshly ground black pepper

Chicken Pittas
Chicken Risotto

1. Dice the chicken in 1-inch (2.5 cm) cubes.
2. Combine the yogurt, lemon juice, paprika, chilli powder, tomato purée and garlic in a mixing bowl. Season with a little salt and pepper, add the chicken and stir to coat. Cover and refrigerate for 30 minutes.
3. Preheat the grill or barbecue. Thread the chicken on to skewers and grill or barbecue for 10–15 minutes, turning frequently, until golden brown and tender.
4. Briefly heat the pitta bread under the grill, turning once.
5. Half fill each warmed pitta bread with equal amounts of lettuce, onion and cucumber. Divide the chicken evenly between the pittas and serve immediately.

Pasta Ratatouille

This makes a delicious and filling pasta meal. By mixing Cheddar and parmesan cheese you will achieve the taste of parmesan for half the cost, as the Cheddar will quickly assume the flavour of the parmesan.

Serves: 4
Preparation time: 40 minutes
Cooking time: 30 minutes
Freezing: recommended for up to 3 months
Selections per serving: 2 Carbohydrate; 1/2 Fat; 1 Protein; 3 1/2 Vegetable; 10 Optional Calories
Calories per serving: 350

(V) if using vegetarian cheeses

8 oz (240 g) courgettes
1 lb (480 g) aubergines
1 tablespoon olive oil
1 onion, chopped
1 garlic clove, crushed
14 oz (420 g) canned chopped tomatoes
2 tablespoons tomato purée
3 tablespoons chopped fresh basil or 1 teaspoon dried basil
8 oz (240 g) spaghetti
2 tablespoons grated parmesan cheese
3 oz (90 g) half-fat Cheddar cheese, grated
salt and freshly ground black pepper

1. Chop the courgettes and aubergines and place them in a colander. Sprinkle them liberally with salt and weight them down with a heavy plate. Leave for 30 minutes to extract the bitter juices and then rinse them thoroughly under cold, running water and drain well.
2. Heat the oil in a large pan and cook the onion for 5 minutes, stirring frequently. Add the garlic and cook for 1 minute more. Stir in the tomatoes, tomato purée and basil along with the drained courgettes and aubergine. Season with a little salt and pepper, cover and simmer gently for 30 minutes or until the vegetables are tender.
3. Meanwhile, cook the spaghetti in a large saucepan of lightly salted boiling water for 12–15 minutes or until just tender to the bite. Drain well.
4. Arrange the spaghetti on a warm serving dish, top with the ratatouille, and sprinkle with the grated parmesan and Cheddar cheeses. Serve immediately.

Beef and Lentil Bolognaise
Pasta Ratatouille

Beef and Lentil Bolognaise

By serving wholewheat spaghetti with this tasty bolognaise sauce you gain extra flavour as well as fibre!

Serves: 4
Preparation time: 15 minutes
Cooking time: 30 minutes
Freezing: recommended for up to 3 months
Selections per serving: 3 Carbohydrate; 1/2 Fat; 2 1/2 Protein; 2 1/2 Vegetable; 10 Optional Calories
Calories per serving: 545

2 teaspoons sunflower oil
2 onions, chopped finely
1 large carrot, sliced
1 courgette, grated
8 oz (240 g) extra-lean minced beef
2 garlic cloves, crushed
1 tablespoon chopped fresh oregano or 1 teaspoon dried oregano
4 oz (120 g) red lentils, rinsed and drained
4 tomatoes, de-seeded and chopped
2 tablespoons tomato purée
5 fl oz (150 ml) beef stock
12 oz (360 g) wholewheat spaghetti
1 teaspoon olive oil
salt and freshly ground black pepper
fresh chopped parsley, to garnish

1. Heat the oil in a large saucepan and cook the onions over a medium heat for about 5 minutes, stirring frequently, until soft.
2. Add the carrot, courgette, minced beef and garlic and cook, stirring constantly, for 5 minutes more.
3. Add the oregano, lentils, tomatoes, tomato purée and stock to the pan. Season with a little salt and pepper, stir well and bring to a boil. Cover and simmer for 30 minutes.
4. Meanwhile, cook the spaghetti in a large pan of lightly salted boiling water to which the olive oil has been added. This should take approximately 12–15 minutes, but follow the instructions on the packet. Drain well and turn into a warm serving dish. Pour on the bolognaise sauce, sprinkle with the chopped parsley and serve immediately.

WW note: combined with the wholewheat spaghetti, the lentils in this recipe help to boost up the Carbohydrate and Protein Selections, making it an excellent source of energy on those days when you could do with a boost yourself!

(V) **Vegetarian option:** use vegetable stock in place of the beef stock and substitute 12 oz (360 g) of quartered button mushrooms for the minced beef. This will reduce the Protein Selection to 1 and increase the Vegetable Selection to 3 1/2 per serving. The Calories per serving will be 485.

Grilled Fish with Provençal Sauce

This tasty dish can be very quick and easy if you make the sauce in advance and reheat it just before serving. It will keep for 2 days in the refrigerator and its flavour will intensify.

Serves: 4
Preparation time: 15 minutes
Cooking time: 40 minutes
Freezing: not recommended
Selections per serving: 1 Fat; 2 Protein; 3 Vegetable
Calories per serving: 210

4 teaspoons corn or olive oil
1 onion, chopped finely
1 carrot, diced
1 small stick celery, chopped finely
2 garlic cloves, crushed
2 teaspoons mixed dried herbs
1 3/4 lb (840 g) canned plum tomatoes, chopped but not drained
1 tablespoon tomato purée
4 x 6 oz (180 g) fish steaks (i.e. cod, halibut or haddock)
2 teaspoons lemon juice
1/2 teaspoon dried basil
salt and freshly ground black pepper

❶ Heat 2 teaspoons of the oil in a saucepan and sauté the onion, carrot and celery for 5 minutes, until softened.
❷ Stir in the garlic and the mixed herbs. Add the chopped tomatoes with their juices and the tomato purée. Season with a little salt and pepper. Cover and simmer for 30 minutes and then remove the lid and boil the sauce rapidly for 5 minutes more, until it has thickened to your liking.
❸ Preheat the grill and line the grill pan with kitchen foil. Arrange the fish steaks on the foil and brush them evenly with the remaining oil. Sprinkle them with the lemon juice and basil and season with a little salt and pepper.
❹ Grill the steaks for 4–6 minutes, turning them once and basting them with the juices. The fish is cooked when it is no longer opaque.
❺ Serve the fish with the Provençal sauce on warm plates.

Cook's note: cod steaks are particularly good in this dish as their firm, white flesh complements the garlic and tomato sauce.

Turkey Stir-fry

The combination of sweet, sour and spicy flavours in this recipe will wake up your tastebuds! Serve with boiled brown rice or wholewheat noodles for a healthy and delicious meal, and don't forget to add the Carbohydrate Selections.

Serves: 4
Preparation time: 20 minutes
Cooking time: 8 minutes
Freezing: not recommended
Selections per serving: 1 Fat; 2½ Protein; 1½ Vegetable; 40 Optional Calories
Calories per serving: 230

1 tablespoon olive oil or sunflower oil
1 oz (30 g) flaked almonds
a bunch of spring onions, sliced
1 red pepper, de-seeded and sliced finely
1 large carrot, cut in matchsticks
1 large celery stick, sliced finely
3 courgettes, sliced diagonally
12 oz (360 g) skinless, boneless turkey, cut in strips
4 oz (120 g) canned unsweetened pineapple slices, drained and chopped with 3 tablespoons of the juice reserved
2 teaspoons light soy sauce
1 teaspoon finely grated fresh root ginger or ½ teaspoon ground ginger
1 tablespoon chopped fresh coriander
freshly ground black pepper

1. Heat the oil in a wok or large frying pan.
2. Add the almonds and stir-fry them for about 1 minute, until lightly golden. Lift them out, using a slotted spoon, and drain on absorbent kitchen paper.
3. Add the spring onions, red pepper, carrot, celery, courgettes and turkey to the wok. Stir-fry over a high heat for 4–5 minutes, until the turkey is cooked but the vegetables remain crisp.
4. Stir the pineapple pieces into the wok with the reserved juice, the soy sauce, ginger and coriander. Season with a little black pepper and cook for 2 minutes more.
5. Sprinkle the stir-fry with the almonds and serve on a bed of freshly boiled brown rice or steaming hot wholewheat noodles.

Cook's tip: prepare all of the ingredients before you begin to cook and make sure that the vegetables are cut in equal-size pieces. This will ensure that they cook evenly – the rest is a breeze!

(V) **Vegetarian option:** substitute 12 oz (360 g) of Quorn for the turkey. This will reduce the Protein Selection to 1½ per serving and the Calories per serving will be 215.

Pork with Black-eyed Beans and Apricots

Serves: 4
Preparation time: 15 minutes
Cooking time: 40 minutes
Freezing: recommended for up to 3 months
Selections per serving: 1 Carbohydrate; 1/2 Fat; 3 Protein; 1 Vegetable; 75 Optional Calories
Calories per serving: 390

15 oz (450 g) lean pork, chopped in small pieces
2 teaspoons sunflower oil
1 onion, chopped
1 red pepper, de-seeded and sliced
2 large celery sticks, sliced
1 tablespoon plain wholemeal flour
1 oz (30 g) dried apricots, chopped
1/2 pint (300 ml) chicken or vegetable stock
1/4 pint (150 ml) dry white wine or dry cider
15 oz (450 g) canned black-eyed beans, rinsed and drained
freshly chopped parsley, to garnish

1. Dry-fry the pork in a hot, non-stick pan, turning frequently until browned all over. Drain and set aside.
2. Heat the oil in a large flameproof casserole dish and sauté the onion, red pepper and celery for 5 minutes. Stir in the flour and cook, stirring, for 1 minute more.
3. Stir in the browned pork, dried apricots, stock and wine or cider. Bring to a boil, stirring constantly, and then cover and simmer gently for 30 minutes, until the pork is tender.
4. Stir the beans into the casserole and cook for 5 minutes more, or until heated through.
5. Sprinkle with parsley and serve immediately.

Cook's note: to chop dried apricots quickly, simply snip them in small pieces with scissors.

Pork with Black-eyed Beans and Apricots

Desserts

For many people, 'dieting' is easy – until it comes to resisting their sweet-tooth. Many a good intention has been foiled by a packet of chocolate biscuits! However, Weight Watchers is not merely a diet, but a way of life, and everybody knows that deprivation does nothing to enhance a life-style. So instead of depriving yourself of that mid-day snack or evening dessert, simply plan it into your daily Selections and feel good, not guilty about what you eat!

If you still think of dessert as being a forbidden pleasure for Weight Watchers – think again, and get ready to taste some truly delicious treats! By reducing the fat content and taking advantage of the natural sweetness of fresh fruits, I've come up with several desserts that both your family and your heart will love you for. Why not pack a slice of luscious Carrot Cake with Sultanas (page 46) into your lunch bag? Or serve your family Gooseberry Fool (below) – they'll certainly be fooled by the custard and whipped cream into thinking that you've gone right off your Programme! And for devotees of the cocoa bean – Chocolate Pancakes with Pears (page 42) will have your guests lining up for their next dinner invitation.

Gooseberry Fool

This creamy dessert has a wonderful flavour and texture and makes a delicious pudding on a hot summer day. If you grow gooseberries in your garden, try doubling the quantities, and then freeze half in a plastic container.

Serves: 4
Preparation time: 15 minutes
Cooking time: 20 minutes + 1 hour chilling
Freezing: recommended for up to 3 months
Selections per serving: 1 Fruit; 1/4 Milk; 1/2 Vegetable; 55 Optional Calories
Calories per serving: 85

1 lb (480 g) gooseberries, topped and tailed
3 tablespoons granulated sweetener
5 fl oz (150 ml) low-fat natural yogurt
3 fl oz (90 ml) canned low-fat Devon custard
3 tablespoons whipping cream, whipped (optional)
tiny sprigs of fresh mint, to decorate

(V)

1. Put the gooseberries in a saucepan with 4 tablespoons of water. Cover and cook gently for about 15 minutes or until the fruit has softened. Alternatively, if you have a microwave, cook the fruit with water in a large covered container for approximately 7 minutes on 100% (full power). Stir and allow to stand for 5 minutes.
2. Using the back of a wooden spoon, crush the cooked fruit to a rough purée – it's better not to sieve or process the fruit as this removes the texture and valuable fibre.
3. Stir in the sweetener and leave to cool to room temperature.
4. Combine the yogurt and the custard in a mixing bowl. Blend in the cooled gooseberry purée and add a little more sweetener if necessary. Spoon the purée into sundae dishes or wine glasses and refrigerate for 1 hour.
5. Top each dessert with a swirl of whipped cream (if using) and a sprig of mint and serve immediately.

Gooseberry Fool

Chocolate Pancakes with Pears

The small quantity of butter used gives the pancakes a delicious flavour without going overboard on the Calories.

Serves: 4
Preparation time: 15 minutes
Cooking time: 20 minutes
Freezing: suitable (for pancakes only) for up to 3 months
Selections per serving: $\frac{1}{2}$ Carbohydrate; $\frac{1}{2}$ Fat; 1 Fruit; $\frac{1}{4}$ Milk; 95 Optional Calories
Calories per serving: 265

$\frac{1}{2}$ oz (15 g) cocoa powder
$3\frac{1}{2}$ oz (105 g) plain flour
1 egg
$\frac{1}{2}$ pint (300 ml) skimmed milk
$\frac{1}{2}$ oz (15 g) butter
2 teaspoons caster sugar
4 fl oz (120 ml) unsweetened orange juice
3 medium-size ripe pears, peeled, cored and quartered
1 tablespoon sunflower oil
a few very thin strips of blanched orange rind, to decorate (see page 10 for preparation instructions)

1. To prepare the batter, first sieve the cocoa powder and flour and place in a food processor with the egg, and half of the milk. Blend until smooth. Stop the machine and scrape down the sides of the bowl. Add the remaining milk and process for a few seconds more. Pour the batter into a jug and let it stand for 10 minutes.
2. Meanwhile, put the butter, sugar and orange juice in a saucepan. Heat gently, stirring, until the butter melts and the sugar dissolves, and then bring to a boil and simmer gently for 2–3 minutes.
3. Add the pear quarters to the saucepan, cover and simmer very gently for about 10–12 minutes, or until the pears are tender.
4. Meanwhile, stir the batter and make 8 pancakes in a small frying pan, using a little hot oil each time, and turning each pancake once until cooked through.
5. Fold each pancake in half and then in half again to form a triangle. Overlap the triangles on a serving plate and serve immediately with the pear sauce.

Chocolate Pancakes with Pears
Hot Baked Bananas with Orange

Hot Baked Bananas with Orange

Bananas taste totally different when they're cooked, and this recipe is wonderfully rich and exotic. Try serving the bananas with a little low-fat fromage frais or natural low-fat yogurt for a very special dessert – of course, you will need to add the extra Selections or Optional Calories!

Serves: 4
Preparation time: 10 minutes
Cooking time: 7 minutes
Freezing: not recommended
Selections per serving: 1 Fat; 1 Fruit; 70 Optional Calories
Calories per serving: 180

(V)

4 small bananas
2 teaspoons lemon juice
1 oz (30 g) low-fat spread
grated zest and juice of 1 medium-size orange
a pinch of ground cinnamon
1/4 teaspoon ground allspice
2 tablespoons rum
2 teaspoons dark muscovado sugar
1 oz (30 g) flaked almonds, toasted

❶ Peel the bananas and brush them with the lemon juice to prevent them from discolouring.
❷ Melt the low-fat spread in a large non-stick frying pan and sauté the bananas on both sides until lightly golden. Transfer the bananas to a warm serving dish and keep them hot.
❸ Place the orange zest and juice, cinnamon, allspice, rum and sugar in the frying pan and bring to a boil.
❹ Cook for 1–2 minutes, stirring constantly, and then pour the sauce over the bananas. Sprinkle with the toasted almonds and serve immediately.

Apple and Blackberry Oaty Crumble

Serves: 6
Preparation time: 20 minutes
Cooking time: 45 minutes
Freezing: recommended for up to 3 months
Selections per serving: 1 Carbohydrate; 1 1/2 Fat; 1 Fruit; 50 Optional Calories
Calories per serving: 240

(V)

1 lb (480 g) Bramley apples, peeled and sliced
8 oz (240 g) blackberries
3 tablespoons Hermesetas Sprinkle Sweet
2 oz (60 g) demerara sugar
4 oz (120 g) rolled oats
2 oz (60 g) wholemeal flour
1/2 teaspoon allspice
1/2 oz (15 g) pistachio nuts, chopped roughly
3 tablespoons sunflower oil

❶ Preheat the oven to Gas Mark 5/190°C/375°F.
❷ Gently mix together the apples, blackberries and Sprinkle Sweet in a 4-pint (2 litre) pie dish or casserole.
❸ In a mixing bowl, combine the demerara sugar, rolled oats, flour, allspice and pistachio nuts. Stir in the oil and mix thoroughly. Sprinkle the crumble mixture evenly over the fruit.
❹ Bake for 40–45 minutes until the topping is lightly golden. Serve hot.

Cook's note: if preparing the fruit ahead, sprinkle the peeled apples with a little lemon juice to prevent them from discolouring.

Bramley Apple Fluff

This mousse-like pudding is very pretty to serve. With their wonderful tart flavour, Bramley apples take on a sherbety taste when combined with the lemon zest, and the fluffy egg-white lightens the dessert to perfection. Suitable for family get-togethers or for more sophisticated entertaining.

Serves: 4
Preparation time: 20 minutes
Cooking time: 10 minutes + cooling time
Freezing: not recommended
Selections per serving: 1½ Fruit; 85 Optional Calories
Calories per serving: 125

(V) if using free-range eggs

1½ lb (720 g) Bramley apples, peeled, cored and sliced
2 oz (60 g) caster sugar
3 tablespoons water
grated zest of ½ lemon
2 egg whites
1 oz (30 g) dried apricots, chopped
blanched strips of lemon rind, to decorate (see page 10 for preparation instructions)

❶ Place the apples and sugar in a medium-size saucepan with the water.
❷ Cover the pan and cook gently, stirring occasionally, for about 10 minutes or until the apples fall to a pulp.
❸ Transfer the contents of the pan to a liquidiser or food processor and purée until smooth.
❹ Pour the apple purée into a mixing bowl and fold in the lemon zest. Set aside to cool to room temperature.
❺ In a grease-free bowl, whisk the egg whites until stiff and carefully fold them into the cooled apple purée. Fold in the chopped apricots.
❻ Divide the apple 'fluff' mixture between 4 sundae dishes and refrigerate until ready to serve.
❼ Decorate with the blanched strips of lemon rind and serve cold.

Steamed Date Pudding

Serves: 6
Preparation time: 15 minutes
Cooking time: 90 minutes
Freezing: recommended for up to 3 months
Selections per serving: 1 Carbohydrate; 1 Fat; 85 Optional Calories
Calories per serving: 245

(V) if using free-range eggs

2 tablespoons rapeseed or olive oil
4 oz (120 g) self-raising flour
2 oz (60 g) wholemeal self-raising flour
2 oz (60 g) dark muscovado sugar
3 oz (90 g) ready-to-eat chopped dates
2 eggs, beaten
grated zest and juice of 1 medium-size orange
1 tablespoon skimmed milk

❶ Lightly grease a 1½ pint (900 ml) pudding basin with a little of the oil.
❷ Mix all of the ingredients together in a bowl, adding just enough milk to create a soft, dropping consistency. Pour into the prepared basin and cover with a double layer of kitchen foil, making a pleat in the centre to allow the pudding to rise. Tie firmly with string.

❸ Transfer the pudding to a heavy-based lidded saucepan. Add boiling water to reach half-way up the pudding basin. Cover and simmer for 90 minutes. Keep an eye on the water level, topping it up with boiling water if necessary.

❹ Remove the pudding from the saucepan and turn it out on a warm serving plate. Serve in slices.

Carrot Cake with Sultanas

This family-size cake is moist and delicious without any sort of topping. The combination of orange juice with cinnamon, sugar and sultanas is wonderful when baked in this yummy American dessert. With its high fibre content, you'll feel satisfied after only a small slice of this admittedly moreish cake, so don't be tempted to go back for a second slice!

Makes: 12 slices
Preparation time: 15 minutes
Cooking time: 50 minutes + cooling
Freezing: recommended for up to 3 months
Selections per serving: 1 Carbohydrate; 2 Fat; 1/4 Vegetable; 90 Optional Calories
Calories per serving: 295

(V) if using free-range eggs

4 fl oz (120 ml) sunflower oil
4 oz (120 g) self-raising flour, sieved
4 oz (120 g) self-raising wholemeal flour, sieved
1 teaspoon baking powder
1/2 teaspoon cinnamon
3 oz (90 g) soft brown sugar
8 oz (240 g) carrots, grated
2 eggs, size 2
grated zest of 1/2 medium-size orange
1/4 pint (150 ml) unsweetened orange juice
3 oz (90 g) sultanas

❶ Preheat the oven to Gas Mark 4/180°C/350°F.
❷ Grease a 2 lb (960 g) loaf tin with a little of the sunflower oil and line the base with non-stick baking parchment.
❸ In a large bowl, combine the remaining oil with the flours, baking powder, cinnamon, sugar, grated carrots, eggs and the orange zest and juice.
❹ Mix well until the ingredients are thoroughly combined and fold in the sultanas.
❺ Transfer the mixture to the prepared loaf tin and bake for approximately 1 hour, until the cake is well risen, golden brown and firm to the touch. Check the centre of the cake with a skewer – it should come out clean.
❻ Cool the cake in the tin for 10 minutes and then turn out to cool until ready to serve.

Carrot Cake with Sultanas
Steamed Date Pudding

Index